wild & rooted: a motherhood collective

The Motherhood Collective

Ashley Randleman
Pamela Henkelman
Gina Meredith
Tracey Crowder
Erica Thesing
Shianne Fisher
Katie Brown

Front cover photo by Cristina Gottardi

Wild: living or growing in the natural environment
Rooted: established deeply and firmly

When we live as the women God has called and created us to be,
we can live and grow wildly.
We can be rooted in who He is and His word, deeply and firmly.

Dear Momma,

You are not alone. I repeat: You are *not* alone. These are words I desperately needed when we first brought home our eight-pound eleven-ounce baby girl, and I still need them today. Motherhood is one of the most challenging, empowering, lonely, enlightening experiences. This is why we need community and encouragement. We need to know that we are not alone. My heart in putting together this project is that mothers—whether first time moms in the thick of the newborn sleep deprived haze or empty nesters who are embracing their grandmother status—realize they have a community of women cheering them on.

This book is written to remind you that you are capable, you are strong, you are called, you are loved, and you are seen. As a mom, I often feel quite the opposite. However, when I find someone else who can look at me and say, "Yeah, I've been there," or, "Hey, I'm there now," it somehow brings light into my solitary darkness and a belief that I can do this. I want the words on these pages to be that for you.

The writers for this project are women who are first time moms still finding their footing, moms of big families, moms of kiddos with special needs, grandmas, and moms in the untraditional sense. The commonalities between all of these women are they love Jesus, they love their families, and they love you.

We pray that as we are led by the Holy Spirit to share our hearts, you, dear sister, may find that encouragement, that sense of community, and that extra push of hope to get you through whatever season of motherhood you find yourself in.
You are not alone. We are in this together.

With love,

Katie

*"When we get together, I want to encourage you in your faith,
but I also want to be encouraged by yours."*
Romans 1:12 (NLT)

We Get to Do This
Ashley Randleman

I always wanted to be a mom. In fact, the thought of not being able to be one had never once crossed my mind.

At the very beginning of time, the human race was commissioned to "be fruitful and increase in number; multiply on the earth and increase upon it" (Genesis 9:7). I simply wanted to take my part in that.

So when I miscarried our first child a few weeks after my husband and I conceived, I was devastated. When it happened again, I doubted if we would ever be able to contribute to mankind.

The doctors wanted to wait until *after my third miscarriage* to run tests on me. However, I didn't think my heart could handle that amount of heartbreak. I believe the Lord knew that as well, so He enabled us to conceive and give birth to our firstborn son, Nathan Alan.

My desire to steward him well was heightened by the dark depths of my pain.

We miscarried again, and then had Josiah Thomas—our fifth pregnancy and second birth.

After Josiah, we had another miscarriage followed by two more babies, Lydia Rae and Titus James. We had found our family.

If you were paying close attention, you noticed the number of pregnancies was eight. I experienced four miscarriages plus the births of our four children that I *get to* raise.

The key words are "get to."

Because there is a big difference between "have to" and "get to."
We often have to do the dishes and laundry but get to go on date night or vacation.

But imagine how our mothering and our marriages would improve if we postured ourselves in a way where all of the "have to"s in our lives were exciting "get to"s?

In Psalm 127:3-5 the blessing of children is made clear:

3 Children are a gift from the LORD;
they are a reward from him.
4 Children born to a young man
are like arrows in a warrior's hands.
5 How joyful is the man whose quiver is full of them!
He will not be put to shame when he confronts his accusers at the city gates.

Since children are a gift, I fully believe we should accept them graciously and enthusiastically.

When something is demanded from someone, it is no longer a gift. It is payment. A true gift is bestowed, not demanded.

My posture of motherhood changed the day I found out I wasn't able to keep my first gift. My entitlement was replaced with brokenness, and instead of demanding a baby from the Lord, I desired a baby from the Lord.

With each subsequent loss and life that followed, my appreciation for the gifts and the rewards the Lord bestowed on me solidified, intensified, and even magnified!

If children were truly a gift, and motherhood was a reward, then I wasn't going to squander my blessing!

I committed in my heart that raising my children would never be a "have to." I decided to always see it as a "get to." And for whatever reason, I haven't been able to shake the thought of the privilege of motherhood—the "we get to."

Privilege is quite simply getting to do something that not everyone gets to do. It's the front-row-seat-V.I.P.-pass-going-beyond-the-caution-tape-and-getting-the-second-helping-first kind of treatment.

And that's what motherhood should look like—even in our painfully long, extremely exhausting, and undeniably overwhelming days.

We've all seen the mothers who behave in a way that suggests they think of their children as curses rather than blessings.

And, upsetting as it is watching those scenarios play out, it always forges a deep desire to do better and to be better because I get to do this.

So, Dear Mommas, whether you planned on being a mom or not, or whether you've suffered loss or not, there is one thing that binds our hearts together: God, the Creator, has given His gifts, and we get to raise them!

So, let's raise them well because "how joyful is the man whose quiver is full of them!" Whether your quiver is one, eight, or twelve, you get to do this.

Surrendered Motherhood
Pamela Henkelman

The buds on the trees burst forth in brilliant green as rainy days envelop the hospital and my heart. I shouldn't be sad holding my newborn son—he is everything we wanted, we love him deeply, and he is even the first grandchild in our family. I should feel joy.

The doctor walks in and says, "How are you today?"

I look outside and sadly whisper, "It's raining again."

As tears roll down my cheeks, he rubs me on the shoulder and gives me a compassionate grin. "It's okay," he says, "it always rains in the spring."

Why am I crying about rain, for heaven's sake? It seems absurd. It's probably just crazy hormones and the stress of major surgery coupled with a lack of sleep. There is nothing like the newborn fog state of being.

Although it's been days since my scheduled c-section, I am not prepared for the pain when the nurse comes in to press on my uterus. Woah!! The pain sears through my abdomen and foreshadows the pain I will later feel at times while raising my kids.

On my fifth day in the hospital, still in the ugly hospital

gown I've worn since my c-section, I ponder important questions like, "Why did I even pack my pretty gown if I can't wear it?" My emotions are all over the place. I feel overwhelmed with everything, including the beauty of my newborn. I could hold him all day long. However, my hubby works in sales, so he needs to be at work and I'm ready to go home.

On the car ride home, I feel especially nervous. I want to scream at every driver, "Be careful, there's a brand new precious, fragile baby in our car! Why are you even on the roads today?" Suddenly I have an alarming thought, which overcomes me with dread and the weight of it all. We are responsible for this little soul. We are responsible to care for this sweet babe. Feelings of doubt, fear, and anxiety weigh on me as I realize the significance of the moment.

Quietly in my heart, I whisper a prayer of surrender: "Jesus, I give you this baby. Help me be the best momma to him, and when I mess up, help me make it right. Guide me, lead me, and help me raise him well. Give me wisdom and strength, grace and joy. Thank you for his little life. I lay him down before you."

Truth be told, I am this baby's momma, but he belongs to God. God has lent him to me for a season. Living surrendered is the wisest thing I can do.

.

It's been almost 31 years since that car ride home.

Over the years, the Lord blessed us with three girls, two boys, and one baby in heaven. They are all adults now, and every season and child required a different sort of surrender.

I have surrendered expectations when days didn't go the way I planned and children didn't make the choices I preferred, and I've surrendered as hot tears flowed, sweet apologies were uttered, and hugs abounded.

I surrendered my dreams and desires to speak and write when God asked me to put them on the shelf until the "empty nest" season. My plans were laid down for the greater good of serving my children.

I surrendered my selfish ways. I learned to serve and honor my husband and kids with healthy meals, a comfortable home, and limitless love and grace. I learned to persevere through sleepless nights, colicky babies, and sick children.

I surrendered my pain. When my children were hurt or they failed. I hurt for them and wanted to fix everything for them, but I understood God is the greater help. I watched my children suffer from bullying and tried to repair their frayed identity as dearly loved and accepted. I helped my kids get through the pain of disappointment, heartbreak, and broken bones. But I had to surrender the outcomes to God.

I surrendered financial goals. I gave up a second income, so I could be home to raise our kids and not pay for daycare. There were no extravagant vacations or the latest electronic toys, but we shared abundant laughter.

I surrendered my flaws. I wanted to be the best mom. My children shaped my character in many ways as my sin was magnified in our interactions. God refined me and made me whole through my children.

Most of all, I surrendered my children's stories. I am not the writer; God is. I don't get to decide how their plots twist or which windy roads they travel. I can't shield them from harm, loss, or their rebellious ways. But I partner with God as I trust His good plans for them.

For all you sweet mommas, Papa knows your heart, and He understands the burden and joy of mothering. The burdens are many, but love is multiplied with each child. Surrender your children, your heart, and your expectations. As the new growth of spring, see what God grows in your family.

Set Apart
Gina Meredith

That's why, when I heard of the solid trust you have in the Master Jesus and your outpouring of love to all the followers of Jesus, I couldn't stop thanking God for you- every time I prayed, I'd think of you and give thanks. But I do more than thank. I ask- ask the God of our Master, Jesus Christ, the God of glory- to make you intelligent and discerning in knowing him personally, your eyes focused and clear, so that you can see exactly what it is he is calling you to do, grasp the immensity of this glorious way of life he has for his followers, oh, the utter extravagance of his work in us who trust him- endless energy, boundless strength!
Ephesians 1:15-19 (MSG)

As moms, we naturally give and give and give. It's who we are. It's our job. Sometimes we get so busy serving, we lose sight of who we were before. In the daily chaos of life, I tend to forget what God says about me. And life has been pretty busy lately. However, everything in my life has been echoing three words. I feel compelled to share these words with you. I need to speak them over your life; Sweet momma, you are *anointed, called, and chosen.*

Webster's Dictionary defines anointed as, "smeared or rubbed with oil; set apart; consecrated with oil." In the Old Testament, the anointing was something that was performed on the outside of the body, but in the New Testament the anointing happens on the inside. John 14:26 says, "But when the father sends the Advocate as my representative- that is, the Holy Spirit- he will teach you everything and will remind you of everything I have told you" (NLT). Ladies, the anointing is a gift! We can use the Holy Spirit in our daily lives! He is our comforter, our breath of life. He desires that we be saturated in His spirit. We are set apart, called, and chosen.

Daughter, He knows your name. He doesn't call you by the labels that others have tried to place on you. Maybe some have said you're not good enough, not creative enough, or not talented enough. Maybe you're not the best cook, but listen to what He says. He calls you lovely, wonderfully made, and child of the king. 1 John 3:1 puts it this way: "See how very much our Father loves us, for he calls us his children and that is what we are!" (NLT)

You are chosen. Ephesians 1:5 states, "God decided in advance to adopt us to himself through Jesus Christ. This is what he wanted to do, and it gave him great pleasure" (NLT). I read that verse and weep with the understanding that God CHOSE me. He didn't question if I was good enough or if I would ever measure up to His standards. He didn't hold back, even though he knew I would fail Him daily. He chose me, and He chose you.

We adopted our fourth child through the foster care system 6 years ago. She was born at 24 weeks and basically left alone in the hospital. She spent the next 23 months in a hospital facility. I'll never forget the phone call asking if we were interested in meeting her. After jotting down over an entire page of notes regarding her medical needs and what the process would look like, my first reaction was, "I'm sorry, but I think we're going to pass." Her social worker asked what my greatest fear was, and after telling her, she said she would call if anything changed. A short time later, she called me back explaining that she was free of her trach. I had no excuse. I agreed to have our family meet her. My husband fell in love with her at that first meeting, while I wrung my hands in anxiety over all the medical needs I'd need to learn to care for and the way this was going to change our lives forever. And it did.

We had to choose to meet our future daughter that day. Then we had to choose to learn and care for her needs, we chose to say yes to her living with us, and we chose to adopt her. Adoption is a choice. God said yes. God hand picked you to fulfill what He has called you to do. YOU are the woman, the wife, the mother for this calling.

Interruptions
Tracey Crowder

I remember a rainy morning that truly changed my life. No catastrophe took place, and no big life event happened. It was just a rainy morning, and I was doing life in one of my favorite roles. I was being a momma. This day I was taking my son to an appointment. The rain stopped as we headed out the front door to go.

If you know me well, you know I think I can get anywhere in just fifteen minutes. That kind of thinking puts me in a crunch at times. This might have been one of those times. Ok fine, I was in a hurry, and I tried to convey to my son, Isaac, the need to hustle it up and get in the car.

What does he do? Instead of hurrying into the car, he ran the opposite direction into the backyard. Frustration rose quickly in this momma.

"Isaac, where are you going? We need to go," I said.

Did he listen? No, of course not. He was clearly captivated by something. Next thing I knew he plopped down on the wet grass. After just getting cleaned up and ready to go, he plopped down on the dirty wet ground! Oh no he didn't.

I was on my way to grab him and give him a personal escort to the car when he said, "Mommy, look. Mommy, look at the butterfly." At this point he was sitting on a rock. Isaac kindly slid over to make room for his momma to sit with him and watch this beautiful monarch. We sat in the wetness of the morning, taking time to notice this beautiful creature in all its splendor. We watched with intrigue as it flew around and entertained us.

Was this an interruption in my day? Absolutely it was. Was I upset about it? At first, I was. Then I realized interruptions are often really invitations to notice.

I think about Jesus and all the interruptions he encountered. One example is the time he traveled to help someone who interrupted his day. On his way, he was interrupted by a woman who had been bleeding for 12 years. No doctor could help her. Then, one day Jesus was walking by, and she just knew in her heart that he was the solution she needed. She thought to herself, "if I could just touch his robe, I will be healed" (Mark 5:28). So with every bit of strength and courage she could find in her, she pressed and pushed her way through the crowd where she finally dropped to the ground. She then stretched her arm out just far enough to touch the hem of Jesus' robe. In that moment she received her healing, strength was restored, and she was finally free from this burden that had plagued her life because Jesus was interrupted.

As soon as she touched Jesus, he felt power leave him, and he took time to seek her out and notice her. This was not a scheduled part of his day. It wasn't on his calendar. She had no appointment. This woman was an interruption that Jesus took as an invitation to notice her. He then encouraged her and commended her for such incredible faith. Yes, even Jesus dealt with interruptions.

If you're a momma reading this, you know all about interruptions. If you're like me, you can't even go to the bathroom without being interrupted.

How many times have you stood in the shower trying to relish the hot water and relax before all the morning crazy begins? Then you hear an exclamation from the other side of the door, "Mom, hey, Mom, Mom!" How many times have you been awakened to crying or vomit? In my case, my baby girl climbs into my bed and twirls my hair into knots while I try to sleep.

Maybe you finally got to schedule a little time for yourself. You have an amazing day planned. Perhaps you'll grab a latte and sit with a book. Maybe you'll go to the salon and pamper yourself. Doesn't that just sound amazing? You have time set aside for you! Then it happens, "Mommy, I don't feel so good." Next thing you know your plans have been interrupted and you're stuck at home with a sick child.

Interruptions happen. Maybe you're in a hurry at the grocery store, and the person in front of you is having that embarrassing moment of being short a few dollars and now they're deciding what to keep and what to put back. You have places to be, and your valuable time is being interrupted.

On the day my son sat in the wet grass to note the beautiful splendor of the butterfly, I learned to take notice. It is a small reflection of the manner Jesus took notice of the woman with the blood condition as his schedule was interrupted. My moment seems minor compared to this incredible miracle moment. Still, the lesson is the same. Sometimes interruptions are invitations to notice. Noticing creates opportunities for special moments, moments to love people and to care about things other than our agendas. I wonder how many enriching life moments we miss because we miss the invitation in the interruption.

Labor In Love
Erica Thesing

"Motherhood is a hallowed place because children aren't commonplace. Co-laboring over the sculpting of souls is a sacred vocation, a humbling privilege. Never forget."
Ann Voskamp

I'm wholeheartedly exhausted. Wholeheartedly.

Labor still.

Firstborn.

I choose to seek an eternal, joy-sculpted hope on this motherhood journey that wholeheartedly co-labors with Christ, His artistic hand in mine, over the life of my precociously creative and wondrously gorgeous-hearted daughter, almost one month into twelve years preteen, Leila Rain.

At the age of not quite two years, her wildflower-esque frame, olive bronze skin, green eyes, glisten and curly hair everywhere self happily inquired on a treasure hunt together, "Mommy, who made this dirt?"

Her theological capacity for mindful expression is a colorful sea of curiosity in the study of God's word, anthropology, music and a soulful voice. She keeps my heart enthusiastically livened with Heaven's intentional wisdom pursuit with her life melody that fashion a spirit humbly surrendered in artful expectancy.

Leila Rain's desire to confidently adventure away from my grasp beats stronger each day as her appetite for knowledge expeditiously devours literature and, likewise, her thoughts center freely on vast dreams in the light of truth beyond her years. My trust is wildly blazoned in the illumination that God is truly her Father and her keeper. The relationship we share is a timely vested gift.

I'm wholeheartedly exhausted.
Wholeheartedly.

Labor still.

Second born.

I choose to seek an eternal, joy-sculpted hope on this motherhood journey that wholeheartedly co-labors with Christ, His artistic hand in mine, over the life of my equally precocious and limitlessly energetic-gifted son of nine and a half years, Laken Jade.

At the age of roughly three, his long surfer-blonde hair, uniquely determined eyes and naturally muscular physique bravely climbed a rope more than ten times his size. He only peered back for a split second to ensure and to encourage his bewildered fan (mother) to courageously cheer a little louder.

Laken Jade's ability to move in boundless energy from one mastered activity to the next is nothing short of astonishing. He bravely competes with a fierce, eye-heart wide open expectancy and fervently esteems hard work as an award to be won in everything he accomplishes. As his mother, I humbly step up my purposeful pace to captivate his heart in motion with Jesus and to be exuberantly present in celebration together on achievement. My trust is heroically positioned in the brilliance that God is his Father and his keeper. The relationship we share is a timely vested gift.

I'm wholeheartedly exhausted.
Wholeheartedly.

Labor still.

Third born.

I choose to seek an eternal, joy-sculpted hope on this motherhood journey that wholeheartedly co-labors with Christ, His artistic hand in mine, over the life of my graciously mature and exuberantly fearless son just shy of four years, Lael Justus.

He has a rare condition presented at birth called

Arthrogryposis Multiplex Congenita that presents extreme physical limitations throughout his body, but his immeasurable spirit defies that. He is most certainly not his confined condition.

At the tender age of seven weeks old, his perfectly dark coiffed hair (blonde now), mysteriously bright brown eyes, and handsomely petite contractured frame dauntlessly withstood his first of many serial casts on his lower extremities. He steadily gazed upward, our eyes locked in unison with a sincere permission to yield tears as a vital and necessary strength. Tears soften our heart steps together on this uncharted journey of medical repertories when the painful climb has proven jaggedly unfair, and they wonderfully wash our fallen skinned soul-knees when fatigued.

Lael Justus's sensitivity of character intent is wisely kinetic as he wholly embraces life with an effervescent; signature smile that happily awakens possibility each day on a missional purpose to love well. His ability to miraculously navigate forward with momentum in a gait uncommon draws the eye attention of many and grants his little voice the opportunity to write a love letter from heaven directly upon the seeker's heart. My trust is relentlessly strengthened in the radiance that God is his Father and his keeper. The relationship we share is a timely vested gift.

I'm wholeheartedly exhausted.
Wholeheartedly.
Labor still.

The Conceited Mom
Shianne Fisher

Talk no more so very proudly, let not arrogance come from your mouth; for the Lord is a God of knowledge, and by him actions are weighed. - 1 Samuel 2:3

Recently I video chatted with my grandma while I cooked hamburger meat for sloppy joes. Growing up in the Midwest, where the Maid-Rite was born, these loose meat sandwiches were often on our family dinner table. The recipe for the meaty filling is pretty simple and typically includes tomato sauce or ketchup, diced onions and Worcestershire. I don't make them often because my husband doesn't really like them, so I was following a recipe I had found online.
You would have thought I insulted my grandmother's entire lineage by not just whipping it up from memory.

"You don't know how to make beef burgers?!" she asked incredulously via FaceTime.

"I do," I said, "I just prefer to follow recipes for everything."

My grandmother, a retired school lunch lady, did not hide the disdain from her face.

But that is who I am: a recipe reader, a researcher, a rule follower. That is how I like to live out most areas of my life. It makes sense to me. There's no room for opinion or second-guessing when the tried-and-true method is out there. Why toy with a recipe when a seasoned chef or culinary expert has already perfected it?

When I became pregnant—surprise!—with our first child, I of course immediately began googling and discovered several ways to do motherhood by the book: natural labor, cloth diapering, exclusive breastfeeding, baby-led weaning, and co-sleeping. I trusted the evidence that, somehow, I would raise up a super baby by following this maternal guide. What I did not anticipate, however, was how these "best practices" might shape my view of other mothers.

Guys, this is ugly. Sin is ugly. Comparison is ugly. But while most of what I read on social media by stay-at-home and working moms alike depicted a postpartum season of mom guilt, I was cruising on my ship of pride—through a sea of poopy diapers, of course. And as my little newborn thrived, she only fueled my ego trip, as if her "success" somehow validated my effort to be Mom of the Year.

Motherhood has been such a blessing. I love my daughter, who is now nearly one-and-a-half and running my house like a queen. But this period has exposed a side of me I never realized existed, a boastful, judgmental, know-it-all. And it didn't matter whether I was actually making anyone else aware of this person. I knew her, and God knew her.

Yet He still loved me. While I wrestled with my feelings of superiority and need to upgrade other people (this sin area is not limited to mothering), His opinion of me did not change. While I inwardly criticized the choices around me, He had already forgiven me. While I touted each parenting win as something I had accomplished on my own, He was drawing me toward Himself. This is why the verse, "For from him and through him and to him are all things. To him be glory forever. Amen," (Romans 11:36) brought me such conviction.

It is so tempting to pat ourselves on the back when our children flourish. When in reality, all the credit belongs to God. Without His strength, wisdom, and grace, I would be a lousy mother —at the very least a self-centered one. When I view this season of littles as a specific calling from and for God instead of a time to collect a motherhood trophy, it allows me to celebrate—not scrutinize—the many different ways of raising a child. When I view my daughter's advances through the Lord's eyes and with a heart of thankfulness, there is no room for comparison.

I have not magically overcome my pride nature overnight. God is refining me in this time at home with my daughter, and I am so thankful for his purifying fire as I strive to be more like Jesus to my family and friends.

While I stand firm on my own mothering choices, I have to daily surrender my infatuation with being right. I have followed friendly advice to "major on the majors" and "minor on the minors" in motherhood and beyond.

I often have to remind myself of the last half of 1 Samuel 2:3 "*by* him actions are weighed." God does not need my help evaluating others. His word is the ultimate measuring rod against which to be measured. I have no authority to gatekeep motherhood. While there is room for encouragement and needed correction among friends, only the Lord knows what is best for each family and whispers those individual truths to us.

It's comforting to know God is with me in this and that he's rooting for me to lay down my self and become more like Him. But I have to believe I'm not alone in this—some of you have overcome or are in the middle of this battle over your mind. I just want to say I am in your corner and know how much of a burden this thought life can be.

And to all the other moms doing your best and struggling with feelings of inadequacy, I want to say I am sorry for judging you from afar. God has chosen each one of us to be mom to our littles for a reason, and our differences only magnify His creative nature. You are enough because God is enough.

Lord, thank you for the gift of motherhood. We praise your perfect design. We admit we often fall short and need your guidance to parent to the best of our abilities. And we repent of our judgmental attitudes toward other mothers. Search us and know our hearts; point out any hidden sin so that we can follow you unhindered and be nothing but encouraging to each other as we raise up our children to know and love you. Amen.

Abundance
Katie Brown

My journey to motherhood hasn't been as dreamy as I thought it would be. About seven months before our four-year anniversary, I was unofficially diagnosed with polycystic ovary syndrome (PCOS). For a month I dealt with mysterious bleeding that led me to my doctor's office. As she proceeded to tell me how difficult getting pregnant would be, there was a knock on the exam room door. A nurse quietly asked the doctor to come into the hallway. The doctor soon returned with a dumbfounded look on her face. She said one sentence that would start the most difficult journey I had ever walked.

"You're pregnant!"

Tears of joy, unbelief, and expectation were shared between my husband and I when I got home and told him. Those tears would soon be replaced with tears of fear, discouragement, and uncertainty. Ten days later, on November 11, 2017, our first precious, beautiful baby left my body and entered Heaven.

I have never felt such a hollow, yet deep pain in all of my life. When it all ended, I felt betrayed. God had promised me a child. I knew He had. Why dangle that hope in front of me only to take it away? I walked around in a broken shell for months. Nothing seemed

right. The big, bright colorful future this child brought was replaced with a gray heaviness that I couldn't take off.
Honestly, I didn't want to. It was all I had left of my child.

But somehow, winter always turns into spring. My heart eventually started to heal along with the barren ground. We began to feel the warmth of the sun outside and in our hearts. Five months later, in April of 2018, we heard those words again. Words that caught our breath and dared us to hope.

"Congratulations! You're pregnant!"

I truly believed we would get to keep this one. God surely wouldn't let this happen again, and so closely together, right? On April 18, 2018, our second child joined their older sibling in heaven. I was numb. I didn't even feel grief. If this was God's plan, if this was pregnancy for me, I didn't want it anymore. I couldn't do it. I know there are many women who have kept trying after several miscarriages, and they are warriors. But I just couldn't do it.

After telling my husband I didn't want to be pregnant again, we began to look at adoption. We knew we wanted a family, but maybe we were meant to have one in a different way. We researched agencies, home studies, and foster care. We went to interviews, talked about expenses, and attended classes. Doors either shut or didn't feel right to open. Little did we know that God was secretly working things together for our good and for His glory.

About a week after our second miscarriage, a woman contacted me and said that God had placed me on her heart. She stopped by my work a few days later with a card. Inside of the card was a hotel gift certificate from a youth workers conference that she and I had both attended in January. Her team won every prize, but they decided ahead of time that they were going to give away whatever they received. She felt led to give the hotel stay to us. Our anniversary was coming up and with our two miscarriages and adoption overload, we needed a retreat.

The first weekend in May we went on our anniversary getaway using the free hotel stay. It was a quiet time of refreshing for both of us. Mother's Day came, and I spent the majority of the day alone, celebrating my babies and trusting that God knew the desires of my heart. During Memorial Day weekend, I began feeling some symptoms that I had felt twice before. Without a doubt I knew what was going on—I was pregnant. I quickly ran up to the local pharmacy, bought a double pack of pregnancy tests and came home. Two positive tests later, we were in hesitant, happy tears.

After some scary moments, some wonderful experiences, and a quick and chaotic delivery, our sweet Emma James entered the world on January 24, 2019. She was a chunky monkey with dark curly hair and was our perfect girl. Let's face it, she still is.

I'm still quite new to this mom thing. I don't think you ever get it fully figured out. But those first months were hard. A blessing? Of course. Life changing? Oh yeah. But mostly, hard. Sleep is the one thing I need in this life, and with a newborn you get very little. My emotions were ragged, my body oddly squishy and foreign, and I had a new life to take care of on top of it.

The devil will take our weaknesses and run with them. Quickly we can go from "Okay, I've got this" to "I am absolutely the worst mom ever." God bless the community of people in my life that remind me of the truth—I am not alone. I can do this. I am the mom that God ordained for Emma. But man, mom guilt can be powerful. When we begin to compare our messy inexperience with someone else's public highlight reel, we can feel less than, empty, and not enough.

Jealousy comes out of scarcity. Generosity comes out of abundance. When I'm exhausted, drained and anxious, I don't have much to give to anyone, especially my husband and child. But, when I give out of abundance, watch out! Our God is the God of abundance.

We don't have to just survive. Motherhood, especially those very early days, feels a lot like just surviving. But we have all that we need (and more!) when we place our foundation on the abundance God has for us. From that abundance we have a footing to pray big prayers for our family and for others. We have what we need to get up *again* to tend to our little ones. We have what we need to *more than* survive.

Jesus said in John 10 that He came that we would have life *and* have it more abundantly. When we operate out of that abundance, we have confidence to be the wives, mommas, women God has called and created us to be. And with that confidence, we can charge Heaven for our family and friends. We can come boldly and constantly to the God of abundance, even at 3am.

As Emma's mom, I am constantly reminded of God's faithfulness. He knew. He knew all along that she would be here. He knew the heartache we would endure along the way. He knew the steps needed to create our specific story. He knows you. He knows your desires. He knows your heart. Psalm 37:4 says, "Delight yourself in the Lord and He will give you the desires of your heart."

The older I get, the more I realize that everything He does is for the good of those who love Him and for His glory. I still wonder why our first two babies went straight to Heaven, but I eagerly anticipate the day I get to hold them in my arms. I wonder why parents have to go through the grief of infertility, loss, and pain. But I know God is faithful. I know He is near. I know He heals, and I know He hears. He is the God of abundance. He is the God of peace. He is the God of your story.

May He show up in the wildest of places to demonstrate His great love for you. You've got this, Momma—not because of anything you can do on your own but because of who God is and what He can do through you. Take a deep breath, make sure your footing is on His abundant foundation, and move forward in His grace.

About the Authors

Ashley Randleman

Aside from Ashley being a pastor's wife, mothering four children, keeping house, homeschooling and working at River Church part-time; her simpler accomplishments are uninterrupted sleep, a complete adult conversation, and the ability to see the bottom of her kitchen sink by the end of the day. She looks forward to date night, cappuccinos, running, and traveling. You can find her at holdingtheplumbline.com where she blogs about "mothering on purpose- with purpose" and on Facebook on Tuesday nights for **Tea at Ten.**

Pamela Henkelman

Pamela is an enthusiastic encourager who writes and coaches women to experience the fullness of their identity in Christ. She has been married to her husband, who is a pastor, for 32 years, and she loves the partnership of leading healthy churches. She's a brand new empty-nester with five adult children ages 19-31. Gigi is her favored term of endearment used by her two grandsons, Teddy and Gus. You can find her writing at pamelahenkelman.com.

Gina Meredith

Gina is a stay at home mom of four. She and her husband enjoy going to the movies and going out on dates as often as they can get away. Gina is in the heart of raising three teenagers and loving every second. Her youngest keeps her on her toes, gives her new perspective, and constantly reminds her how blessed she is. She can often be found frequenting the Caribou drive thru for her favorite coffee while shuttling her kids around.

Tracey Crowder

    You will often find Tracey sipping on cinnamon coffee, laughing loudly, and leading a parade of little people. She is a hairstylist, a worship pastor, and leader of multiple businesses with her husband. She has mothered 20+ children through the foster care system. They have adopted four children and are currently in the process of adopting a sibling group of three. She passionately pursues James 1:27, which says, "Religion that God accepts as pure and faultless is to look after the orphans…" Their family enjoys living life to the fullest and chasing their God given dreams. They strive to make the world a better place one day at a time.

Erica Thesing

Erica is a reflective thinker, a childlike dreamer, and a Christ wonderer. Planted in Central Iowa with a transitional heart between city and country life, she is a mother to three adventurously willed children and a wife to her wisely devoted husband. She desires to creatively paint hope in the colors of redemptive promise with surrender-full words. She loves to stylistically adorn and curate a space through a whimsical lens of exposed compassion that guides the littlest to the eldest of these to gather in a summery embrace of grace.

Shianne Fisher

Shianne is a former journalist and a current stay at home mom to one little girl. She enjoys snuggling close for a good movie, playing board games with her friends, and watching green things grow. Her cat, cleaning, and coffee are a few of her favorite things. These days you'll find her at the playground or library, but she misses her old stomping grounds, the hot yoga studio and climbing gym. Her greatest desire is that her life would reflect the love of Jesus and advance His kingdom.

Katie Brown

Katie is married to her best friend, James. They live with their beautiful daughter and two precious pups in Iowa. She enjoys doing yoga, drinking Earl Grey tea with honey, and baking. Katie loves Jesus and is thrilled to bring others together in literary, spiritual, and creative ways. You can find a collection of her writings at heykatiebrown.wordpress.com.